CRAFT TOPICS

WORLD WAR II

FACTS ● THINGS TO MAKE ● ACTIVITIES

RACHEL WRIGHT

FRANKLIN WATTS

LONDON•SYDNEY

© 1994 Franklin Watts
This edition 2001

Franklin Watts
96 Leonard Street
London EC2A 4XD

Franklin Watts Australia
56 O'Riordan Street
Alexandria, Sydney, NSW 2015

ISBN 0 7496 4197 5

Editor: Hazel Poole
Design: Sally Boothroyd
Artwork: David McAllister
Photography: Peter Millard
Additional picture research: Juliet Duff
Consultant: Diane Atkinson

A CIP catalogue record for this book is
available from the British Library

Printed in Dubai

CONTENTS

COUNTDOWN TO WAR

At 11.15 a.m. on 3 September 1939, Britain's Prime Minister, Neville Chamberlain, make the following radio announcement:

"I am speaking to you now from the Cabinet Room at 10 Downing Street. This morning the British Ambassador in Berlin handed the German Government a final note, stating that unless we heard from them by 11 o'clock that they were prepared at once to withdraw their troops from Poland, a state of war would exist between us. I have to tell you that no such undertaking has been received and that consequently this country is at war with Germany."

Adolf Hitler and Nazi generals.

In 1933, Adolf Hitler came to power in Germany as leader of the Nazi Party. Under his command, the Nazis began to increase the size of their armed forces and to build new weapons of war. In 1938 Hitler challenged the treaty even further by taking control of Austria and Czechoslovakia, two of Germany's neighbours to the south. On 1 September 1939, he moved his troops into Germany's eastern neighbour, Poland. Having failed to prevent this invasion by peaceful means, Britain and France then declared war on Germany.

Everyone was given a gas mask at the start of the war, just in case the Germans dropped poison gas on Britain. As it turned out, the gas menace never happened.

The outbreak of war did not come as a great surprise to many of those who listened to that broadcast. After losing the First World War (1914–1918), the defeated Germans were made to sign the Treaty of Versailles. This said that Germany would have to pay for damage caused during the war, and it could no longer have a huge army or any submarines, tanks or warplanes. Many Germans thought the terms of this treaty too harsh, particularly those who belonged to the National Socialist or Nazi Party. Ruthless and racist, the Nazis gained support by promising to smash the Treaty of Versailles and make Germany rich and powerful once more.

THE PEOPLE PREPARE

Britain had begun to prepare for war well before Germany's invasion of Poland. As early as 1935, local authorities were urged to prepare plans for reducing the damage and casualties that would be caused by an air attack. By the time war actually broke out, millions of gas masks had been issued to the public, and nearly 1 1/2 million people, mainly children, had been sent from the major cities, which were most likely to be bombed, to the safety of the countryside.

During the blackout the only outdoor lights in many British cities were the searchlights used to spot enemy aircraft.

LIGHTS OUT!

The blackout began two days before the war actually started. Under blackout rules, everyone had to cover up their windows at night with black material. This was done to make it more difficult for German bomber planes to find their target in the dark.

The blackout was a real nuisance. Street lamps were turned off, which meant that pedestrians often bumped into each other. Traffic accidents were common because car headlights had to be blacked out, and deaths from drowning increased as people fell off bridges or walked into ponds.

LEAVING HOME

MEN AT WAR

Family life changed dramatically with the outbreak of war. All fit young men had to leave home and join the army, navy or air force. This was known as the "call up". At first only fit men aged between 20–22 had to register for the call up, but in time this age limit was extended to include men aged between 18 and 41.

Men in "reserved occupations", such as coal miners, engineers and scientists, did not join the forces because their jobs were considered important in wartime. Like those not fit enough to enter the forces, men in "reserved occupations" also worked as volunteer fire-fighters, ambulance drivers and Air Raid Precaution (ARP) wardens. (ARP wardens helped to look after bombed out survivors and also made sure that the blackout rules were obeyed.)

During the war, British men were sent to fight in Africa, the Far East and Europe. Some of them were away from home for so long that their children and relatives did not recognise them when they returned.

WOMEN AT WAR

In December 1941, women aged between 19–30, without young children or husbands living at home, had to register for war work. After 1943, women up to the age of 50 were expected to register too.

Women who joined the forces were mostly employed as secretaries, drivers, cooks and mechanics. Those not in the forces helped to make up for the shortage of men by working in factories or on farms, railways and buses. Lots of women also volunteered to work as part of the Women's Voluntary Service. Their duties included providing meals and drinks for survivors and rescue workers.

WOMEN OF BRITAIN
COME INTO THE FACTORIES
ASK AT ANY EMPLOYMENT EXCHANGE FOR ADVICE AND FULL DETAILS

Posters were used throughout the war to encourage people to help the war effort.

CHILDREN IN WARTIME

For many children living in Britain's cities or industrial areas, the toughest part of the war was leaving their parents to go and live with strangers in the countryside. Many of the children who were evacuated at the beginning of September 1939 had never been out into the country before. Some were rather afraid of the unfamiliar animals that they saw. Others were surprised to find that apples grow on trees. Lots of children from Britain's city slums were also amazed to find themselves staying in houses with inside toilets, hot running water, clean sheets and carpets.

Poor evacuees were not the only ones to be amazed. Some better-off country families were horrified to find that many of the children from the cities had head lice, skin diseases, ragged clothes and dishonest habits. Similarly, evacuees from wealthier homes were often shocked to find themselves in tiny, dirty houses where they had to do all the housework.

These evacuation experiences did have some good effect, though. They made people more aware of how others lived, which forced the government to take action to help those living in Britain's slums.

Most children were evacuated in school groups with their teachers. They wore name tags, in case they got lost, and carried their gas masks in cardboard boxes slung over their shoulders.

Some evacuees remained in danger areas because their parents refused to have them evacuated.

At first the war seemed unreal to those in Britain. Although there was some fighting – mostly at sea – there were no heavy air raids or poison gas attacks on Britain, as expected. In fact, by January 1940, many evacuees had returned home. This strange period, known as the Phoney War, did not last long though. In the spring of 1940, the Nazis stormed their way into Norway, Denmark, Holland, Belgium and Luxembourg. By the summer, they had invaded France as well.

Following the fall of France, Britain (and its colonies) was left with two choices. It could either ask for peace, or face Hitler's troops alone. Guided by Winston Churchill, who had replaced Neville Chamberlain as Prime Minister in May 1940, Britain decided to stand up to Germany – and Germany decided to invade Britain.

ANTI-INVASION TACTICS

With the threat of invasion hanging over their heads, the British acted quickly. Posters were put up telling people not to spread gossip that might be helpful to an invader. Arrangements were made for church bells to be rung as an invasion alert. And some coastal towns in S.E. England were declared evacuation areas because it was thought that the Germans would land in these places.

"LET US GO FORWARD TOGETHER"

▲ Winston Churchill's brilliant, rousing, patriotic speeches helped to lift people's spirits.

HOME HELP

In May 1940 the British Government asked men aged 17–65 to enrol as unpaid part-time soldiers. The response to this appeal was stunning and by the summer over one million men had volunteered to join what became known as the "Home Guard". Some of these men joined up because they wanted to help the war effort but they were either too young, old or unfit to be in the regular armed forces. Others had not joined the forces because they did jobs which were vital to the war effort.

Home Guard units worked hard to protect Britain from German parachute attacks. They kept a lookout for enemies and spies, guarded factories and airfields, and took down signposts and place names which might have been helpful to enemy parachutists landing in Britain. By doing all this, the Home Guard left professional troops free to carry out more essential duties.

▲The Home Guard was nicknamed "Dad's Army" because some of its members were rather old.

The removal of signposts confused many British road users. Those who got lost were not often keen to ask the way in case they were mistaken for spies. ▶

MAKE A TIN HELMET

Like many people who did war-work, members of "Dad's Army" sometimes wore tin helmets to protect their heads. To make a similar helmet . . .

You will need: a round balloon
- a tape measure ● felt pens ● scissors
- a piece of cardboard ● calculator
- a pair of compasses ● craft knife
- newspaper, torn into strips ● ruler
- fungicide-free wallpaper paste
- cocktail stick ● fine sandpaper
- cutting board ● matt emulsion paint
- a strip of thread elastic ● poster paints ● petroleum jelly

▲ Two boys pretending to be armed soldiers.

▲ **1.** Measure around the top of your head, as shown, and add 2 – 3 cm to this measurement.

▲ **2.** Blow up the balloon and ask a friend to hold the tape measure around it, just above the middle.

▲ **3.** Very slowly let some air out of the balloon until it is the same size as the measurement you took in step 1.

▲ **4.** Knot the end of the balloon. Put the tape measure around the balloon again and hold both steady while your friend lightly draws a circle to mark the position of the tape measure.

5. Divide the measurement you took in step 1 by 6.28. Set your pair of compasses to this measurement and draw a circle on the cardboard.

6. Draw an outer circle, about 4 cm wider than the first. Cut out both circles.

▲ **7.** Smear a thin layer of petroleum jelly over the top of the balloon, down to the pen line. Push the cardboard brim up to the line.

8. Attach the brim to the balloon by pasting small strips of newspaper around the join.

9. Cover the top of the balloon with a layer of unpasted newspaper. Cover the brim with a layer of newspaper, pasted on one side. Add at least one other layer of pasted paper to the balloon and brim and leave to dry.

10. When dry, trim your helmet, rub it down gently with sandpaper and paint the outside with emulsion paint. When the emulsion has dried, paint the helmet again using poster paints.

▲ **11.** Using the craft knife, make two pairs of crosses in opposite sides of the brim, and open them up with the cocktail stick. Thread the elastic through all four holes and knot the ends together.

BOMBS OVERHEAD

BATTLE OF BRITAIN

Hitler knew that unless Britain's Royal Air Force (RAF) was kept out of the skies, his invasion fleet could not cross the English Channel in safety. So, to protect his troops, he ordered his own air force to destroy the RAF, its air bases and aircraft factories. This campaign was not a success though, for during the summer of 1940, the RAF took to the skies and beat off the German air assault.

This aerial combat, which saved Britain from a Nazi invasion, is known as the Battle of Britain. Chilling and thrilling, it was watched by thousands of people in southern England, including A. Hodgson, who wrote this newspaper report.

"I was one of hundreds of Londoners who stood in the streets cheering as two bombers were sent hurtling to destruction by our fighters yesterday. Thousands of feet above us we watched a terrific battle as fighters and bombers dodged in and out of the clouds. In a clear patch of blue sky I watched a bomber roar along with a fighter hard on its tail. Machine-guns rattled as the fighter swooped after it. For a few seconds we watched a thrilling air duel. Then the bomber almost stood on its nose in mid-air, came hurtling down in a death dive and blew up before it reached the ground. The pilot baled out and we watched him slowly glide down."

The Blitz started on 7 September 1940 and continued on and off until the middle of May 1941. Bombs continued to fall on Britain after this period, but not as constantly as during the Blitz.

Children watching the Battle of Britain. The bits of aircraft and shell splinters that fell to the ground were eagerly collected by schoolboys for their wartime collections or scrapbooks.

THE BEGINNING OF THE BLITZ

Germany's failure to wipe out the RAF was partly due to a mistaken change of tactics. In September 1940, the Germans started to bomb Britain's cities instead of RAF air bases in the hope that Britons would panic and accept defeat. This campaign of terror bombing became known as the Blitz. It caused children who had returned home in 1939 to be evacuated again, and brought many non-military people right into the heart of the war.

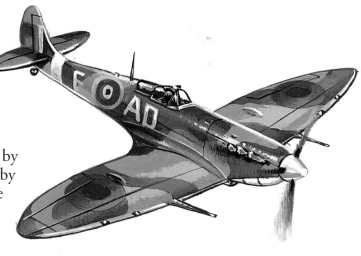

A number of RAF pilots flew Supermarine Spitfires similar to the one shown here in the Battle of Britain.

UNDER COVER

At first, German bombers attacked by day and by night. Then they came by night. As soon as these aircraft were spotted in the night sky, air raid sirens sounded to warn everyone that an air raid was about to start. Some families ran down to a communal brick and concrete shelter in their street. Others sheltered from the bombs at home, either down in their cellars or underneath a table or the stairs. Many people just stayed in their beds! Families with a garden often went outside to hide in a dark and damp shelter made from corrugated iron. These were known as Anderson shelters.

Anderson shelters were often covered with earth.

LIFE UNDERGROUND

The most obvious place of shelter for many Londoners was their nearest underground railway station. At first conditions underground were very uncomfortable, but as the war wore on, bunk beds, toilets and snacks were provided to make life more bearable for the shelterers.

Like the other types of shelter on offer, these stations were not 100% safe. In January 1941, a bomb fell above Bank underground station, killing over 100 people sheltering below.

PICKING UP THE PIECES

As soon as a raid was over, a siren sounded the "all clear" and people went outside to see how much damage had been done. Some discovered that their homes had been flattened. Others found that their friends and relatives had been injured or killed. On 10/11 May 1941, German bombers dropped 708 tons of bombs on London alone, killing 1,400 people and badly injuring 1,792 others.

During the Blitz the Germans showered Britain with a deadly mixture of exploding bombs, fire bombs and delayed-action bombs. Together these posed huge problems for the police, fire-fighters, bomb disposal experts, ambulance drivers, first aid parties, ARP wardens and other professional and voluntary helpers.

"BUSINESS AS USUAL"

At first people found preparing for air raids and the clearing up afterwards exhausting and time-consuming. But as the war continued, many people adjusted their lives to take account of the Blitz and they continued to earn a living.

Rescue services worked long and hard putting out fires and bringing bomb survivors to safety.

On finding that their shop fronts had been blown out, many London shopkeepers simply put up a sign saying "More Open Than Usual", and carried on working. Shared experiences like this often brought friends and neighbours much closer together.

Over 30,000 people were killed in Britain during the Blitz.

▲The bombing of houses left many people homeless for a while.

▲ A bomb-damaged building.

◀ A milkman sets off on his round through rubble-strewn streets, not knowing whether the houses at which he is to deliver are still standing.

The Blitz ended in May 1941 when Hitler turned the full might and fury of his air force against his new enemy, Russia.

ON THE FOOD FRONT

Before the war, as today, a wide variety of foods were brought into Britain by ship. Some of these foods were imported because they couldn't be grown in Britain. Others were produced in Britain, but not in large enough quantities to feed the whole population. During the war, however, the British Government had to reduce both the amount and variety of food it imported. This was because shipping space was needed for raw materials to make weapons, and German submarines were also attacking ships bringing foods from abroad.

Not surprisingly this cut-back left certain foods, such as sugar and butter, in short supply. So, to ensure that these scarce foods were shared out fairly, the government issued everyone with a ration book.

Ration books were full of coupons, which could be cut out and used to buy a fixed amount of rationed foods each week or month. Every time a housewife bought some sugar, for example, she had to give a sugar coupon to her local shopkeeper. When she had used up all her sugar coupons for one week, she had to wait until the following week before she could buy any more sugar.

Rations varied throughout the war as foods became more or less plentiful. The list below gives you an idea of how much rationed food an adult was allowed per week.

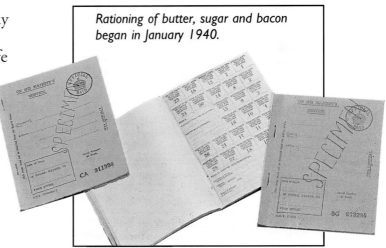

Rationing of butter, sugar and bacon began in January 1940.

Shoppers often had to queue up for hours to buy rationed foods. ▼

100g bacon and ham
1 shilling and tuppence
(6 pence) worth of meat
250g fat (including butter)
50g cheese
1800ml milk
225g sugar
50g jam
50g tea
1 egg
88g sweets
(Egg powder, dried milk, canned fish and dried fruit were also available in rationed quantities)

Changes in food supply during the war meant that most British people were healthier in 1945 than they had been in 1939.

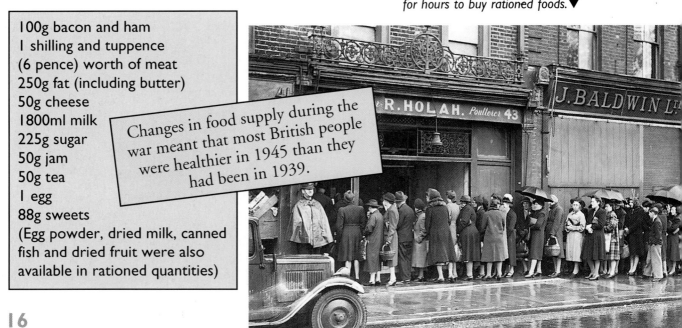

POTATO PETE AND DR. CARROT

Certain foods from abroad, such as bananas, oranges and apricots, were very difficult to buy during the war. Potatoes, carrots and other foods which grow well in England, however, were easier to get hold of, and cartoon characters called Potato Pete and Dr. Carrot appeared on leaflets, telling people to eat plenty of these foods.

The slogan "Dig For Victory" appeared on posters and banners, encouraging people to help the war effort by growing their own food. In response to this appeal, farmers ploughed up more land to grow extra wheat, barley, oats and potatoes. Local councils dug up parks and sports fields in favour of vegetables, and city and townspeople turned their gardens into vegetable plots and started to keep hens and rabbits.

DOCTOR CARROT guards your Health

I'm an Energy Food!
Says POTATO PETE

To make up for the shortage of "exotic" fruits, some adventurous housewives made banana sandwiches using parsnips and banana essence.

▲ Even bombsites were dug over and used for growing food.

FAKE FLAN

With familiar foods in short supply, the government came up with some imaginative suggestions for substitute ingredients in recipes. The wartime recipe below shows you how to make an apricot flan . . . without any apricots.

To make the oat-flavoured pastry

You will need: 150g self-raising flour • 50g butter • 50g rolled oats • salt • 450g baby carrots • almond essence • 4 tablespoons plum jam • sieve • about 8 tablespoons water • knife • fork • two mixing bowls • rolling pin • pastry board • wooden spoon • small saucepan • 22-cm flan dish • grater • serving spoon with drainage holes

▲ **1.** Turn on the oven at Gas Mark 7, 220°C, 425°F. Grease the inside of the flan dish with a little butter.

2. Sift the flour into one of the mixing bowls. Add a pinch of salt.

▲ **3.** Cut the butter into small pieces and rub it into the flour with your fingertips until the mixture looks a bit like breadcrumbs.

4. Add the oats and about 4 tablespoons of water.

5. Mix with the knife and then with your hands until you can lift the pastry out in a ball.

▲ **6.** Sprinkle some flour over the pastry board. Roll out the pastry and use it to line the flan dish. Trim any ragged edges with the knife.

▲ **7.** Prick the base of the pastry with the fork. Then put the pastry case in the oven, near the top, for 15–20 minutes until it is firm and golden brown.

Wartime cooks often made oatmeal pastry because it didn't use too much fat, and it contained oats which were easy to buy.

To make the filling

▲ **8.** Wash and trim the carrots. Thinly grate them into the second bowl.

▲ **9.** Add a few drops of almond essence and 4 tablespoons of jam. Pour in 3–4 tablespoons of water and mix everything together with the wooden spoon.

▲ **10.** Put the mixture in the saucepan and cook it over a low heat until the carrots are soft.

▲ **11.** Using the serving spoon, put the carrot mixture into the pastry case and leave to cool. Serve cold.

CARROT CON?
According to the government's Ministry of Food, the carrots in this recipe taste a bit like apricots.

CLOTHES IN CRISIS

DON'T TAKE THE SQUANDER BUG WHEN YOU GO SHOPPING

Like food, petrol, soap and clothes were also rationed during the war. Clothing rationing began on 1 June 1941. Everyone was allowed a basic 66 clothing coupons a year, which more or less added up to one complete outfit.

Shop-bought clothes, made during the war, were designed to use as little material as possible. Men's trousers were not allowed to have turn-ups and suit jackets could only have one row of buttons. Hems and seams had to be narrow and even the width of a collar and the number of pockets allowed on a garment had to be kept to a minimum.

◀ *As the war continued, shoppers were urged not to waste anything. The government's symbol for waste was a creature called the "Squanderbug".*

Those who could afford it sometimes took their old clothes to a professional dressmaker to have them altered. ▼

MAKE DO AND MEND

With new clothes much harder to come by, women were encouraged to repair and remake their family's old clothes. Unwanted cardigans were unravelled and reknitted into something else. Old curtains and tablecloths were cut up and made into skirts and other garments. Even knitted dish cloths could be sewn together to make a cheap sweater.

For fashion-conscious women, life in wartime Britain must have been a nightmare! Military uniforms and high-street fashions were not very glamorous, and make-up and stockings were hard to find. Because of the shortage of stockings, some women drew a line down the back of each of their legs to look like a stocking seam. Others dyed their legs with gravy browning, which had the unfortunate effect of attracting flies on a hot day.

SCRAPS AND BONES

Old clothes were not the only things to be remodelled during the war. Housewives were asked by the government to hand in their unwanted aluminium pots and pans, so that they could be melted down and turned into aeroplanes. They were also asked to put spare paper and cardboard aside for recycling, and to save bones, so that they could be turned into glycerine for making explosives. Most households also saved left-over food for feeding farm animals.

◀ *Campaigns urging people to recycle goods probably helped to keep everyone's spirits up. This was because these campaigns made non-military people feel that they were contributing directly to the war effort.*

RADIO DAYS

As most people in Britain didn't have a television set until the 1950s and 60s, everyone relied on the radio during the war to keep them entertained, informed and educated. Comedy and music programmes were very popular, as were the regular news bulletins.

"Each evening at 9, everyone stops . . . for the evening news. It is almost an offence to telephone at the hour of the BBC bulletins and as you walk along the pavements the announcer's voice echoes through all open windows."

Cecil Beaton, photographer, 1944.

FACT AND FICTION

Reading books became a much more popular pastime during the war, and despite paper shortages, publishers managed to print some new titles. Newspapers were keenly read too, even though journalists had to be careful about what they wrote. The full truth about enemy attacks was often not printed, in case it depressed people.

THEATRES OF WAR

In September 1939, the government closed Britain's theatres and cinemas because it thought that it was a bad idea to let crowds gather in case there was an air attack. This decision was quickly overturned though, when it became clear that it was cheaper to keep an audience warm in a cinema on a cold night than it was to keep each member of the audience warm in their homes.

Although some cinemas were bombed and many people badly hurt, cinema-going was hugely popular during the war. In fact, some people were so film-crazy that they refused to leave their local cinema when the air raid sirens sounded because they wanted to find out how the film ended.

Live performances were also popular during the war because, like films, they

Wildly romantic and exciting, 'Gone With the Wind' helped to take cinema-goers' minds off the grim reality of war.

helped to cheer everyone up. Concerts were staged in factories to entertain war workers, shows were put on in underground stations to amuse those crowded on the platforms, and famous entertainers travelled far and wide to perform for the troops.

SPORTS CUTS

When war broke out, most familiar sporting events came to an end. Many professional sportsmen joined the forces or police and some football clubs lost their grounds. Yet, despite these setbacks, sport was not given up completely. Football, for example, was reorganised into regional leagues so that footballers could play in a team near to where they were stationed or working. Watched by local supporters, these matches helped the war effort by keeping the players fit and the spectators cheerful.

Concerts staged in tube stations helped to while away the time for those sheltering underground.

SONGS OF WAR

Although all forms of entertainment suffered during the war, new songs continued to be written and sung, both on the radio and in live concerts. Sometimes proud and defiant, sometimes sad and quietly hopeful, many of these new songs matched and formed the public's mood. Slow, emotional numbers such as "We'll Meet Again" and "I'll Be Seeing You" were particularly popular because they put into words and music what many people parted from their loved ones felt.

British singers, George Formby (right) and Vera Lynn (below) worked hard to entertain people during the war. Known as the "Forces Sweetheart", Vera Lynn often sang songs about hope and determination in times of trouble.

Written in 1939, "We're Gonna Hang Out the Washing on the Siegfried Line" is a jokey song which reflects the confidence many Britons felt at the start of the war. (The Siegfried Line was a system of fortifications along part of Germany's western border.)▶

◀ Rich and energetic, the music of big American 'swing' bands, such as Glenn Miller's Army Air Forces band, was also popular during the war. The Americans entered the war in December 1941, and in many ways helped to change popular British culture.

Like other American performers, the comic actor Bob Hope helped to entertain US troops. ▼

GOT ANY GUM, CHUM?

Dancing was one of the most popular pastimes during the war, and from 1942 onwards British dance halls were filled with American servicemen.

America came into the war officially in December 1941, after Germany's ally, Japan, bombed an American naval base at Pearl Harbour in Hawaii. American troops and weapons were then sent to Britain to help prepare for an invasion of Nazi-occupied Europe.

America's servicemen were better dressed than those from Britain. They were also better paid, which meant that they could afford to be generous with the cigarettes, sweets, chewing gum and stockings that the U.S. army brought over from America. Understandably, many British girls were swept off their feet by "the yanks" and about 60,000 girls married American servicemen.

▲ A young couple dancing a popular wartime dance called the "jitterbug".

▲ The North American P-51 D Mustang was a fighter plane, used to protect U.S. bomber planes.

British troops were helped by men from German-occupied countries, as well as by servicemen from Britain's colonies and the Dominions. Unlike the Americans, some of these men stayed in Britain after the war.

FLY A U.S. FIGHTER PLANE

1. Trace all the templates on page 27, including the dotted lines. Turn the tracing paper over, lay it on the 150gsm paper, and scribble over the outlines with a pencil.

You will need: tracing paper
● pencil ● craft knife ● scissors
● 150 gsm cartridge paper
● sticky tape ● coloured pencils
● ruler ● small lump of Plasticine
● cutting board ● 1 small paper clip

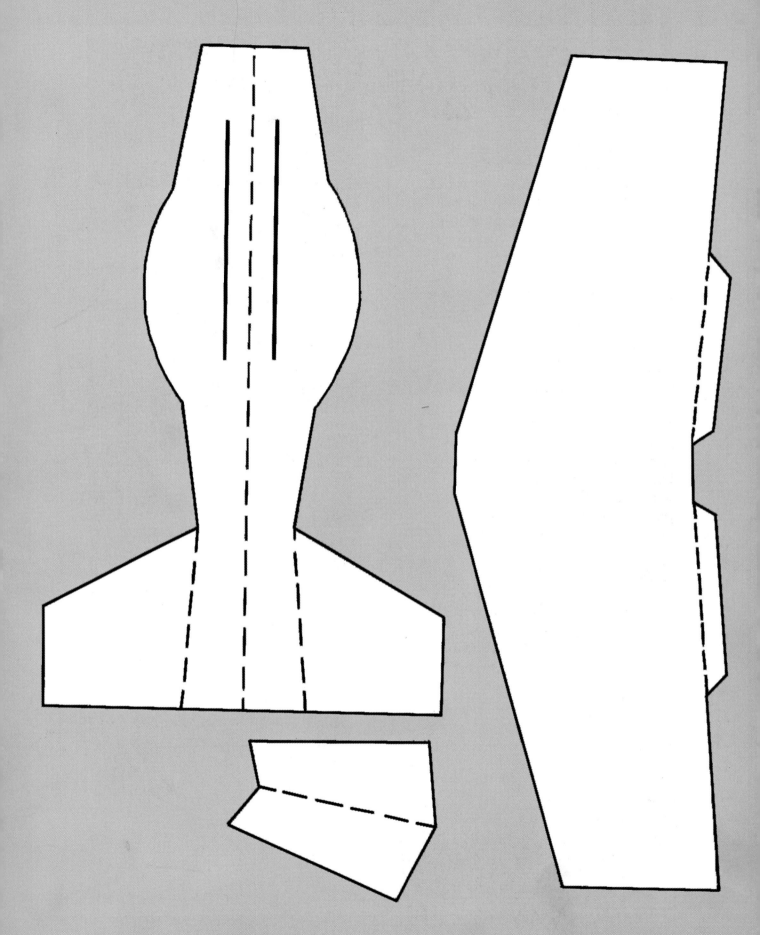

▲ **2.** Cut out all three paper shapes. Then gently run the tip of your craft knife along the dotted lines, using the ruler to guide you.

▲ **3.** Cut out the slits on the fuselage, using the craft knife and ruler, and colour the plane.

▲ **4.** Fold down the wings' ailerons and slot the wings into place. Secure the wings underneath with a little sticky tape, if necessary, and check that they are at the same angle.

PAPER PILOT'S TIP

● If your plane nose-dives too quickly, remove a little Plasticine.

● If it swoops upwards and then dives, add a bit more Plasticine.

● Fly your plane in a room without breakable objects.

▲ **5.** Fold down both parts of the tail and check that they are level with each other. Re-position the wings' ailerons so that they slope downwards.

▲ **6.** Fold the tail fin in half and tape it into place, fold first, as shown. It should point straight up.

▲ **7.** Slide a paper clip onto the nose of the plane and fold a little Plasticine around it.

8. To fly your Mustang, hold it under the wings, point its nose slightly downwards and launch it gently.

VICTORY IN EUROPE

On 6/7 June 1944, British, American and Canadian troops invaded France, to free Europe from Nazi control. By 7 May 1945 Germany's defences were in ruins, and the Nazi Supreme Command had surrendered.

Victory in Europe Day (VE Day) was celebrated on 8 May 1945. Public buildings were fully lit up for the first time in years and people held parties in their street.

Adolf Hitler committed suicide on 30 April 1945.▼

Young children saw their first bonfires and firework displays and lots of war-weary households flew Union Jacks and other Commonwealth flags from their homes. The celebrations went on all night. For those who had lost family or friends during the war, these celebrations must have been tinged with sadness.

8 May 1945. VE Day celebrations in Trafalgar Square, London. The Second World War didn't finally come to an end until 2 September 1945, when Japan formally surrendered.▼

VICTORY OVER GERMANY 1945

GIVE THANKS BY SAVING

GLOSSARY

Air raid – an attack by bomber planes.

Air raid siren – a machine which made a loud wailing noise, to give warning of an air raid.

Ally – a friend, partner or helpmate. Great Britain, France and America were allies during the Second World War because they fought on the same side.

Blitz – short for "blitzkrieg", a German word which means lightning war.

Colony – a state or country which is controlled by a more powerful country.

Dominion – a self-governing country of the British Commonwealth. The British Commonwealth is a group of countries that are or were once ruled by Britain. Australia and Canada are part of the British Commonwealth.

Evacuate – to move from a place of danger to a place of safety.

Evacuee – someone who is moved from a dangerous area to somewhere safer.

Invasion – an attack by one country on another.

Import – to bring something into a country.

Jitterbug – an energetic type of dancing to jazz music which was popular during the Second World War.

Nazi – a member of Germany's National Socialist Party.

Patriot – someone who loves their own country.

Racist – someone who believes that their own race of people is better than others.

Rationing – a system for sharing out scarce goods in fair portions.

Serviceman – a member of a fighting service.

Yank or Yankee – a British nick-name for someone from the United States of America. In America, 'Yankee' is often used to describe someone from the northern United States, as opposed to the southern.

LACES TO VISIT

Here are just a few of the museums in Britain which have displays showing what life and weaponry was like in the Second World War.

Cabinet War Rooms
Clive Steps
King Charles Street
London
SW1A 2AQ
Tel: 071-930 6961
A personal sound tour takes you through the 21 underground rooms from which Churchill and his Chiefs of Staff organised Britain's war effort.

Duxford Airfield
Duxford, Cambridge
CB2 4QR
Tel: 0223 835000
This former Royal Air Force Station houses the largest collection of military and civilian aircraft in Europe, as well as military vehicles.

HMS Belfast
Morgan's Lane
Tooley Street
London
SE1 2JH
Tel: 071-407 6434
HMS Belfast, Europe's largest preserved warship from the Second World War, is now a floating naval museum.

Imperial War Museum
Lambeth Road
London
SE1 6HZ
Tel: 071-416 5000
The Imperial War Museum has large displays covering the First and Second World Wars. It also offers the dramatic "Blitz Experience" which takes visitors back to the days of the Blitz.

Museum of London
London Wall
London
EC2Y 5HN
Tel: 071-600 3699
This museum has a gallery showing what life was like for Londoners during the Second World War.

Royal Air Force Museum
Grahame Park Way
Hendon
London
NW9 5LL
Tel: 081-205 2266
In addition to hearing Churchill speak and seeing some legendary Second World War aircrafts, visitors to the RAF Museum can undergo the "Battle of Britain" experience.

Watford Museum
194 High Street
Watford
Hertfordshire
WD1 2HG
Tel: 0923 232297
Watford Museum has a small gallery devoted to the topic of Watford at War. It includes displays about civil defence, rationing, air raids, and the Watford Home Guard.

Welsh Folk Museum
St. Fagans
Cardiff
CF5 6XB
Tel: 0222 569441
This museum has, among other things, a small country post office, refurbished to represent the period around 1943, plus an Anderson shelter.

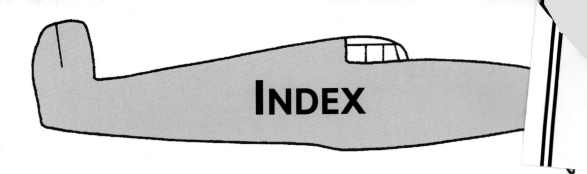

INDEX

Additional Photographs:
Bridgeman 18; Camera Press 29; e.t. archive 6, 10, 19, 23; Hulton Deutch 4, 6, 17, 22, 25; Imperial War Museum 22; Popperfoto 4, 7, 11, 14, 18, 19, 29; Topham 12, 16, 17, 25, 26.